Children Won't Wait

Helen M. Young

Brownlow

Calligraphy by
Faith Scarborough

Original text copyright 1985
by Helen M. Young

Supplemental text copyright 1988
by Paul C. Brownlow
ISBN: 0-915720-83-3

Brownlow Publishing Company, Inc.
6309 Airport Freeway, Fort Worth, Texas 76117

Foreword

*G*od has entrusted you with a precious gift—a child. You have been chosen to love him, nurture him, train him, and guide him to become a free and independent adult. Yours is a ministry of love.

What a priceless heritage you are providing your child in bringing him into a family where he is wanted, where love is waiting for him, and where he can feel accepted and secure.

In this delightful blessing, *Children Won't Wait*, Helen M. Young urges us to give our child our best: The best of our time, our mind, our attitudes, our affection, our faith. She writes as a parent to parents. She has known the pressures and distractions of other urgent calls, but sees parenting as the important call.

And don't forget how brief the time is—only eighteen years—to love and guide him. I pray that you will fill these fleeting years with understanding, happy comradeship, loving discipline, and that nothing will cause you to neglect this God-given task which no one can do as well as you.

God Bless you,

Dale Evans Rogers

Other Brownlow Gift Books

A Special Gift

For:

Becky

From:

Diane

March 22   *1995*

There is a time to anticipate
the baby's coming, a time to
consult a doctor;
A time to plan a diet and exercise,
a time to gather a layette.
There is a time to wonder at the
ways of God, knowing that
He guides our every step.
There is a time to dream of what
our children may become.
A time to pray that God will teach
us how to train the children
that He gives.
A time to prepare ourselves that we
might nurture this new soul.
But soon there comes the time
for birth,
For babies won't wait.

There is a time for night feedings,
for colic, for baby tears.
There is a time for rocking and a
time for walking the floor.
A time for patience and self-sacrifice,
A time to show our children that this
new world is a world of love
and goodness and dependability.
There is a time to ponder what a
child is — not a pet nor toy, but a
person, an individual — a soul
made in God's image.

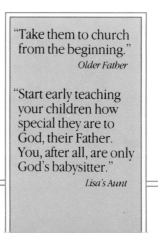

"Take them to church
from the beginning."
Older Father

"Start early teaching
your children how
special they are to
God, their Father.
You, after all, are only
God's babysitter."
Lisa's Aunt

There is a time to consider our stewardship. We cannot possess another human being.

Our children are not ours. We have been chosen to care for them, to love them, to enjoy them, to nurture them, and to answer to God.

We resolve to do our best for them. For babies don't wait.

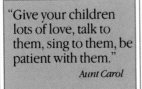

"Give your children lots of love, talk to them, sing to them, be patient with them."

Aunt Carol

"You raise what you praise."

Sarah's Mother

"Practice family traditions with your children. Be sure to include them in old traditions as well as in developing new ones."
Parent of Teenagers

There is a time to hold them close
and tell them the sweetest story
ever told;
A time to show them God in earth
and sky and flower, to teach
them to wonder and reverence.
There is a time to leave the dishes,
to swing in the park,
To run a race, to draw a picture,
to catch a butterfly, to give them
happy comradeship.

"Don't be afraid to say
NO to something your
child wants. They don't
need everything they
ask for at Christmas.
They don't have to
have a room full of
toys to be happy. Many
times they would
rather have Mom or
Dad just sit down and
play a while rather
than have a lot of toys
to play with alone."

Greg's Babysitter

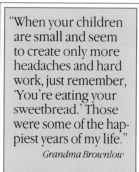

"When your children are small and seem to create only more headaches and hard work, just remember, 'You're eating your sweetbread.' Those were some of the happiest years of my life."

Grandma Brownlow

"Help your children
establish their own
individual faith in
God and His Son."
Johnny's Grandpa

here is a time to point the way, to teach their infant lips to pray, To teach their hearts to love God's Word, to love God's day, For children don't wait.

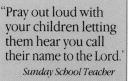

"Pray out loud with your children letting them hear you call their name to the Lord."
Sunday School Teacher

"Teach your children to hang on to God, while they are small, and when they are old, they won't let go of His hand."
Emily's Babysitter

*There is a time to sing instead
    of grumble, to smile instead
    of frown,
To kiss away the tears and laugh
    at broken dishes.
A time to share with them our
    best in attitudes — a love of
    life, a love of God, a love of
    family.
There is a time to answer questions,
    all their questions,
Because there may come a time
    when they will not want
    our answers.*

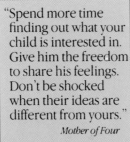

"Spend more time
finding out what your
child is interested in.
Give him the freedom
to share his feelings.
Don't be shocked
when their ideas are
different from yours."

Mother of Four

"Continue talking to your children as they grow older. Also, continue hugging them."

Parent of a Teenager

*There is a time to teach them
so patiently to obey, to put
their toys away.
There is a time to teach them the
beauty of duty, the habit of
Bible study, the joy of worship
at home, the peace of prayer,
For children don't wait.*

"Tell your children
they are special and
have a special purpose
in life."

Monica's Mom

"Be consistent in
treatment (regarding
discipline — don't
punish something one
time and next time let
it ride)."

Andrew's Aunt

*here is a time to watch
them bravely go to school,
to miss them underfoot,
And to know that other minds
have their attention, but
that we will be there to
answer their call when
they come home,
And listen eagerly to the story
of their day.*

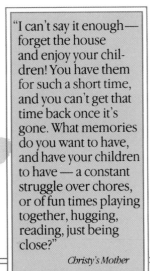

"I can't say it enough—
forget the house
and enjoy your chil-
dren! You have them
for such a short time,
and you can't get that
time back once it's
gone. What memories
do you want to have,
and have your children
to have — a constant
struggle over chores,
or of fun times playing
together, hugging,
reading, just being
close?"

Christy's Mother

*There is a time to teach them
independence, responsibility,
self-reliance.
To be firm but friendly, to discipline with love,
For soon, so soon, there will
be a time to let them go,
to try their wings,
For children won't wait.*

"Remember your child
is a child and not an
adult. He needs your
guidance, love, and
discipline."

Grandma

"Keep a sense of
humor. Don't take
yourself too seriously."

Uncle Bob

*There is a time to treasure
every fleeting minute of
their childhood.
Just eighteen precious years
to inspire and train them.
We will not exchange this
birthright for a mess of
pottage called social posi-
tion, or business success
or professional reputation.*

"Spend more time with
your children doing
simple family things."
Jordan's Father

"If I had it to do over
again, I would be more
demonstrative of my
love for them and not
take for granted that
they knew I loved
them."
Mother of Five

*An hour of concern today
may save years of heart-
ache tomorrow,
The house will wait, the dishes
will wait, the new room
can wait,
But children don't wait.*

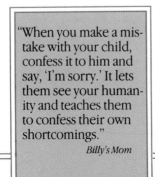

"When you make a mistake with your child, confess it to him and say, 'I'm sorry.' It lets them see your humanity and teaches them to confess their own shortcomings."

Billy's Mom

*There will be a time when there
will be no slamming of doors,
no toys on the stairs, no childhood
quarrels, no fingerprints on the
wallpaper.
Then may we look back with joy and
not regret.
There will be a time to concentrate
on service outside our home;
On visiting the sick, the bereaved, the
discouraged, the untaught;
To give ourselves to the "least of these."
There will be a time to look back and
know that these years of love were
not wasted.
We pray there will be a time to see our
children upright and honest souls,
loving God and serving all.*

"Teach your children early that people are more important than things."

Sandy's Grandmother

*od, give us wisdom to see that
today is the day with our children.
That there is no unimportant
moment in their lives.
May we know that no other career is
so precious,
No other work so rewarding,
No other task so urgent.
May we not defer it nor neglect it,
But by thy Spirit accept it gladly,
joyously, and by thy grace realize
That the time is short and our time
is now,
For children won't wait!*

"Do not expect perfec-
tion, but instead com-
pliment and praise
their efforts when
they do their best."
Grade School Teacher

God's Babysitters

Guidelines for helping your children grow physically and spiritually strong.

As you know by now, babies do not arrive with instruction manuals. It is left to you as a parent to be creative in developing ways to comfort and guide your child into adulthood. Much of it will come naturally to you; but from the day your baby is born, you will be flooded with advice from family and friends concerning the best way to raise this gift that God has given you. Those who offer you their words of wisdom are well-meaning; they have usually been down the parenting road before and realize the importance of these initial years in shaping your child's future. What they may not fully comprehend is that each parent and child has a unique style of relating to the world and each other, so parenting techniques that work for one person may not always work for another.

Please keep in mind that for both you and your baby, the road to becoming an adult is an exciting, frequently frustrating and sometimes frightening adventure.

The real struggle for you as a parent will not be in encouraging your child's development. As long as you understand how to react to the various stages, he will mature naturally. The biggest concern to most Christian parents is that as he becomes independent of your constant care, he will also become more dependent upon the Lord. The best way to nurture your child's spiritual faith is to display it yourself from the time your child is born. *Be* what you want your child to *become.*

It is never too early to begin modeling Christian behavior. Because every child develops at a different rate (independent of IQ), perception of certain spiritual qualities may begin before anyone expects them to. And there is no doubt that the peace of God that surrounds your life can be appreciated by the youngest of infants even if it is not understood until later.

The following guidelines are designed to help you understand the physical and emotional stages your child will go through. It is important to consider these issues along with his unique temperament and personality when deciding upon the best way for *you* to guide your child into a life founded upon Christian principles and a strong faith in God.

Birth to Two Months

The first few steps of this developmental journey will occur during infant bonding. For the baby, bonding is his first and most important relationship. For the parent, bonding is a relationship made up of many levels of love and responsibility.

Bonding occurs while the parent is meeting the child's physical needs. For example, rocking and cuddling when feeding, cooing, smiling, singing and talking when bathing or changing the infant are all bonding activities.

Bonding is an emotional attachment developed with the child through eye contact, hugging and the tone of voice that says, "I am listening. I am here and will always be here. You are worthwhile." While crying is your child's only way to communicate his needs to you, his ability to receive and interpret communication is much greater.

He understands more than you realize. And soon you will be able to understand each of his crying signals: from hunger to wanting to be held. At this early age, it's important to respond to his cries in order to make him feel secure. He is still too young to really manipulate you; so comforting should not spoil him, but bring the two of you closer together.

The sense of security developed during this time is crucial and carries into adulthood. Infants who do not experience loving, bonding relationships, will find it much more difficult to give and receive love later in life as adults.

During this early period, begin (if you have not already started) praying for your child's spiritual development and for God to help you as a parent. As your child grows, pray with him and for him so that he can hear you. Let him hear you thank God for him and ask God to bless his life daily.

Two to Three Months

Soon, you will begin to notice that your baby spends more time looking at you as opposed to strangers. He concentrates on your face since the distance at which he focuses best is about twelve inches, or the distance from your arms when you are holding him. Soon he will be able to recognize you by looks alone and begin to smile in response to your smile — a trait that will make you fall in love with your baby all over again.

Your child will also become a more active participant in interactions. He will attempt to get your attention and engage you in play by making funny faces and cute noises. He will also begin adjusting to your sleeping and eating patterns by resting through the night and feeding more regularly and less frequently, which should put both of you more at ease.

Most parents are good at telling and showing their children that they love them, but don't forget to begin telling them that God loves them too. Teach them about God's love and forgiveness by displaying those qualities yourself.

Four to Five Months

Around this age your baby will start to babble and coo as well as smile in response to your presence, so playtime takes on a more conversational quality. Your baby may also begin to laugh, although it is not completely clear why. Children of this age tend to giggle at things they don't really understand, while things that are too confusing will make them cry. Whatever the reason, laughing helps to form an emotional bond between you and your child. This activity also builds confidence in your baby because adults tend to repeat actions that provoke laughter, which helps him gain more control over his environment.

As you continue praying for and with your child, also begin to look at books — Bible story books and other kinds. Another fun way to help young children understand God's presence in your life is to sing Christian songs to them and with them. Even if they are too small to understand the words, the melody will help them remember the message until they are able to comprehend the meaning.

Six to Twelve Months

Your baby has now developed his vision and memory skills well enough to distinguish visually between different faces. Since your child is comfortable with and dependent upon you, the ability to distinguish between people may cause "stranger anxiety" to develop. There are wide variations in the onset of this phase, just as there are variations in the strength of the reactions. Some children become hysterical and cling to their parents at the sight of an unfamiliar face, while others may simply give the stranger a look of uncertainty.

Stranger anxiety may peak, seem to disappear, then reappear again and again over the next year. This depends upon your baby's experiences, temperament and method of handling new situations. Making your baby feel secure and exposing him to many people may help to reduce his fear of strangers, but it is important to understand that your baby's anxiety is a healthy reaction and part of his normal emotional development.

When your baby's fear of strangers is at its peak, you may be tempted to sneak out when you want to leave him with a babysitter. However, this may make him more upset. Forewarning children about what is going to happen next is often a useful technique in reducing fear and distress reactions.

Until a child develops "object permanence," he believes that objects he cannot see do not exist. When you leave the room, it is as if you no longer exist. Your baby's protest is a healthy reaction. This "separation anxiety" represents his fear of losing you and does not mean he will become an overly dependent adult.

Surprisingly, games like "Peek-a-Boo" help him in this separation of self from you. To a young baby, when you cover up your face, you really have disappeared. When you uncover your face, you magically return and the infant's surprise and joy of being reunited are very real. In future months, when your toddler covers his face, he believes you cannot see him since he can't see you, but he understands that no one actually disappears. This discovery may help lessen his fear of losing you, but his dependence upon you will always cause some anxiety during separation until he is old enough to trust in your inevitable return.

During this six- to twelve-month period, your baby will begin to crawl, and as he does, he will use you as a secure base from which to explore. He will cling to you tightly at first, but then he will start to move away to check things out and return for an occasional hug and reinforcement. Your support of his exploration by being available but not interfering unnecessarily in his activity is important in his learning how to control the environment. The best way to allow for safe, independent exploration is to child-proof your home by removing hazardous or breakable objects from your baby's reach. Then relax!

Twelve to Eighteen Months

By twelve to eighteen months, your child begins to understand that you are a distinct entity (whether you wear a dress or jeans, you are still the same person). As he develops greater motor control, he can move away from parents and see them at a distance, which helps him to perceive himself as a separate individual, and he begins to develop a sense of self.

During these months, your child will also begin to walk; and, oddly enough, this may cause some conflicting emotions. On the one hand, his first steps move him toward independence as if to say, "See what I can do." On the other hand, as he reaches and grabs for you, he seems to say, "Don't leave. I need you every moment." All of this is normal and healthy. The best you can do is be there to encourage his efforts and reassure him.

When walking and playing outside, this is a natural time to talk about God and creation. Give God the credit for all the flowers, grass, trees, etc. This will help your child become familiar with all God has made and given him to enjoy. It will also increase his growing respect and love for God.

You may also notice that during this period your child has developed a specially loved blanket or stuffed animal that he takes to bed and "frightening" places with him. This is called a transitional object because it helps in the transition from extreme dependence upon you to independence, providing security and comfort in your absence. It is important to respect your child's desire for this object. In most cases, he will outgrow the need for it and give it up when he is ready.

Eighteen Months to Two Years

Language makes life a lot easier. When your baby can communicate some of his feelings to you verbally, your job becomes much more clear. You can ask what's wrong; you no longer need to be a mind reader. Even one word in combination with gestures can mean whole sentences to you. Encourage him to use his natural ability to acquire language by insisting that he ask for what he wants rather than just guessing what he would like and giving it to him. One extremely intelligent girl did not speak until she was four because her family allowed her to point out what she wanted and they provided it. Encourage your child to speak; don't be too good at reading his signals.

For some children, knowing what the words are but not being able to say them correctly can be very frustrating. They have so much to express, but they don't know how to say it. Try not to put too much pressure on them to pronounce words correctly. At this age, they are trying to master many things at once. Gentle encouragement and assurance are all that are needed at this time.

If you feel that something is wrong with your child's language development or that he is not listening to you, check with your pediatrician. Babies prone to excessive ear infections may have some hearing loss which delays language development and causes subsequent behavioral problems.

At eighteen months, your child views events differently from you; he has an egocentric view of the world. In essence, he sees himself as the center of all activity and is unable to understand another person's perspective. This means that he cannot comprehend what someone else may be feeling, so the concepts of sharing or showing compassion are underdeveloped at this age. Therefore, parents should not get upset over what appears to be selfish behavior.

Besides your baby's self-involvement, you will notice that one of his first and favorite words is *no*. At this stage, defiance is definitely the name of the game. Temper tantrums are also common; and while they are disruptive and embarrassing, they are a part of growing up. This opposition is his way of stating independence and is a very important developmental step.

Like many areas of development, it is difficult to predict exactly when this stage will surface. Some children have a better grasp of language, so defiance may be diffused by talking with the parent. At other times, discussion won't help because the child simply will not give in. When this happens, it is important for both parents to sit down together, without the child, and discuss what is worth fighting the child for and what isn't.

These selfish and defiant behaviors are in no way a rejection of your Christian values or of your child's emerging spiritual development. This is not proof that your child is going to become a "savage heathen." Try to keep in mind that these difficult times are necessary for your child to separate himself from you and move toward becoming a distinct individual.

Difficult behavior may also be caused by other complications. Due to the child's recently increased motor activity, sleep patterns may be disrupted. So much time is spent walking and running that when bedtime comes, he may be too tired to go to sleep easily. He may also wake up with night fears. At this age, your child can't distinguish between fantasy and reality. Nighttime, being alone and dreams can all be very frightening. The best that you can do is comfort him by letting him know that you are there to protect him and that God will watch over him.

However you decide to deal with his anxiety, it's important for you to be consistent. Developing a regular bedtime routine such as reading to him before he goes to sleep is comforting to the child and good for his emotional growth and cognitive development. Reading Bible stories to him is a wonderful way to share some quiet times together, build his faith and develop good habits.

Children at this stage become upset when activities such as bedtime are disrupted. If a situation arises in which a routine must be changed, let the child know what to expect so that the transition can be easier. In short, your role during this developmental phase is to balance the toddler's desire for independence with his continued need for reassurance, love and affection.

The Third Year
The first half of the third year may remain difficult for you and your child as he struggles for independence. The best any parent can do is try to keep from becoming frustrated and screaming "No!" all the time. If you can remain calm and reinforce positive behavior with praise, hugs and kisses, you and your child will both survive this developmental phase.

By the time your child reaches three years of age, many changes have occurred. It is important to begin talking to your child about how he feels. He has a full range of emotions and with your help can learn to label and understand them. He may also have replaced you with a child as favorite playmate even though he still needs and desires your love and support. Your child no longer views the world as filled with magical powers. Cause-

and-effect relationships are becoming apparent to him as well as flaws in his parents' armor. Before this stage, his parents were perfect, and now they're simply human. This realization is good for the child as long as you are honest in sharing your weaknesses with him — it can only draw you closer together.

Being completely honest is important for many reasons. One of the ways you can show your child that God keeps His promises is for you to be honest and keep *your* word. Honoring promises may be difficult when uncontrollable circumstances arise, because children do not understand *exceptions.* For this reason, it is important that you promise as little as possible and keep the promises that you do make. Substituting the phrase "We'll try to" may be a wise decision when pressed for a commitment.

As your children become old enough to understand choices, let them see that you consider God's will when making decisions. There's no better way to show them how God affects their lives at a very personal level and that He only wants the very best for them. This is how they learn to incorporate abstract Christian principles that they've heard about in Bible stories and songs into their own unique and very important lives.

Children are a wonderful gift from God and are worth any amount of time and effort needed to help them grow physically and spiritually strong. God has given you a special blessing: the opportunity to take part in the miraculous development of your child's mind, body and soul. Treasure these moments forever by creating cherished memories rather than lingering regrets, for *Children Won't Wait.*